The Microlearning Guide to Microlearning

By Carla Torgerson, MEd, MBA

Carla Torgerson
Torgerson Consulting
www.torgersonconsulting.com
©2016
Iteration 1.0
ISBN# 978-0-692-80667-8

Why I Wrote This Book

One day I was talking with my friend, Megan Torrance, the owner of Torrance Learning. I was telling her how I wanted to write this book, but I wasn't quite sure what to say or how to get started.

She asked if I'd read her book. I grimaced a bit. "Well, uh… I *have* your book, but I haven't exactly had time to read it yet." I said. Although Megan is always understanding, I still felt like maybe I should fake a call on my cell phone and duck out of the room.

But I didn't—and we had a great conversation about my ideas and goals. Little did she know that she also helped me to realize the importance of a book that could be read in brief chunks, something that had great applicability, but wouldn't take a ton of time for people to read.

Ultimately, this is the book I would actually read to the end. And I hope it's the same for you.

How to Use this Book

If you look at my bookshelf you'll see all kinds of great books in neat rows, most of them with a bookmark part way through. This is my moment of truth—I must admit that I don't read nearly as many professional books as I'd like.

But in my defense, I'm busy. So are you. That's why I'm writing this guide to microlearning in bite-sized chunks. Every page has just one micro idea, and they are numbered so you can find them again easily. Flip through, jump around, even skim. You should be able to read this book end-to-end and pull out the lessons you need in just a little time.

In fact, here's my goal for you: 15 to 20 minutes. Yes, a whole book in 15 to 20 minutes. Within these pages are my best tips and advice for creating a microlearning program. Flag the ones that make the most sense for you and try them in your next project. Refine them and revise them to work for you. Then come back and find some more tips as you continue to hone your skills with microlearning.

And then let me know how it goes! I'm always looking for feedback and suggestions! **You can reach me at carla@torgersonconsulting.com.**

Acknowledgements

I've been lucky to be surrounded by amazing people, both personally and professionally. Without those people, this book would never have been possible.

To my husband, Thomas Wortman—your encouragement and support have been instrumental, not only to this book or my career in general, but also to my growth as a person. You are the best thing that's ever happened to me and I don't know what I'd do without you. I love you more than you know.

To the rest of my family... my son, John, who enables me to see the world through fresh eyes every day. My mom and dad, Len and Jennette Torgerson, and my brother and his family, Trevor, Haylee, Mackenzie, and Griffin Torgerson. Although we're miles apart, I still carry with me the lessons all of you have taught me over the years.

Professionally, there have been tons of people who have been critical to my journey and to whom I am deeply indebted. I know I'll miss somebody, but here's a stab.... First, to all the folks I had the privilege of working with at Allen Interactions, but especially Dr. Michael Allen, Julie Dirksen, Ethan Edwards, Edmond Manning, Linda Rening, Laura Nedved, Susan Quakkelaar, Sam Mattson, and Chris Vostmyer. All of you shaped my instructional design thinking in tangible ways.

An extra special mention goes to Julie Dirksen, author of *Design for How People Learn*, and owner of Usable Learning. I have learned so much from you over the years. I still remember that semester when we took nearly every Saturday to design a college class on effective teaching. We used to joke that I helped you with your side project for the pizza, but we both know that the pizza didn't matter. I worked on that project because I learned so much from working alongside you all those Saturdays. You are one of the smartest instructional designers I know, and one of my professional heroes; you reached for the stars and you made it!

Megan Torrance—I still remember that fateful day in Orlando when I was two hours from a meeting to pitch my new course ideas to the

Association for Talent Development (ATD) ... you helped me find clarity in a bunch of ideas, and enabled me to nail that meeting. You don't know how much you influenced my early work in microlearning, nor that you were the catalyst that spurred that work and this book. For both of those I'm extremely indebted. Thank you.

Courtney Vital Kriebs, Vanessa Fludd, and Jason Sturges—you and the rest of the ATD team have been a great support, and provided important guidance as I was developing my microlearning work. You also gave me opportunities that have led me to where I am now.

Jen Hoeke—my amazing friend and graphic artist. You took my ideas (I can't even call them sketches) for the MILE model and turned them into something amazing. But you've done that so many times over the years; you always make my designs make sense (and look good!). I'm a better instructional designer when you're in the room. There was no better person to partner with on my microlearning work and this book, and I'm grateful that you agreed to help with all of this.

My current work family (in no particular order): Jamie, Jonathan, Roz, Theresa, Nicole, Mike, Alexis, Brenda, Valanie, Laura, Stephanie, Tim, and Dan. You've all been there to talk through ideas, and have given me flexibility to pursue my professional dreams.

A big thank you to John Sadowski—you had such a powerful influence on my work and my thinking ... and on my confidence when I needed it most. You left this world far too soon. I miss you often, and wish you were still here to influence my microlearning work. I know this book would have been better for it.

And to the thousands of instructional designers across the nation that I've had the pleasure of talking with in classes or presentations or as clients over the past ten or more years. I have learned from each and every one of you.

Carla Torgerson
December, 2016

About the Author

Carla Torgerson, MEd, MBA, has more than 15 years of experience as an instructional designer and instructional strategist. She has taught classes for ATD, the Association for Talent Development, on eLearning, mobile learning, and microlearning, across the country for the past 10 years. Her long relationship with ATD is a testament to her excellent teaching skills and outstanding participant evaluations.

Carla has consulted with numerous *Fortune 500* clients including McDonald's, Netflix, Facebook, Twitter, Adobe, Express, Kellogg, The University of Phoenix, Fidelity, Cargill, Medtronic, Merck, and Best Western. She has designed solutions ranging from $15,000 to more than $2 million.

She has worked as a senior instructional designer at Allen Interactions, a leader in eLearning design, and as a senior instructional strategist at Maestro, a leader in mobile learning. Currently she is a senior instructional designer and internal consultant at Spectrum Health, a large organization with more than 24,000 employees, where she designs and develops training primarily focused on developing leadership skills and business acumen. She has been exploring microlearning for the past few years, and developed MILE, the MIcroLEarning Design Model©.

Carla has a Master of Education (MEd) focused in technology-based education. She also has a Master of Business Administration (MBA), which helps her to see training through a business lens. She has authored numerous blogs and articles, including a chapter in Michael Allen's *2012 e-Learning Annual*.

Find out more:
http://www.torgersonconsulting.com/

Or connect on LinkedIn:
https://www.linkedin.com/in/carlatorgerson

Table of Contents

What is microlearning?

Micro Idea 1

Microlearning is a piece of learning content that can be consumed very, very quickly. Some people define microlearning as being as short as 90 seconds. Others go as high as 10 minutes.

Micro Idea 2

I define microlearning as a piece of learning content that can be consumed in no more than five minutes. I base this on research on the Modern Learner from Bersin by Deloitte; they found that most learners won't watch videos longer than **four minutes**.

Micro Idea 3

Let's say you want to learn something new in Microsoft Word. You could watch a two minute video on YouTube, a ten minute video on your LMS, or go to a one hour in-person class. **Which would you choose?**

Micro Idea 4

As with any teaching medium, it's dangerous to be too firm about rules regarding length. I've seen outstanding microlearning resources that were two minutes long, and other excellent ones that were eight minutes. I've also seen microlearning resources that were shorter than two minutes that felt like a waste of my time.

Micro Idea 5

Microlearning can be presented in any digital medium—typically text, infographic, mini eLearning, or video.

Micro Idea 6

The best guidance regarding length and format is to ask yourself what **you** would want. Would you give up your time in a busy day for this learning?

Why is microlearning so hot right now?

Micro Idea 7

Microlearning really isn't new. eLearning has gotten progressively shorter over the past ten years, and the idea of learners getting content when they need it has been around even longer. Even the earliest software had help menus, and job aids are nothing new. Performance support really started with Gloria Gery's work in the early 1990s—more than 25 years ago!

Micro Idea 8

A convergence of three factors make microlearning the most popular kid on the block right now: the proliferation of mobile phones, our social connectedness, and everyone's very busy schedules.

Micro Idea 9

The biggest factor driving microlearning is mobile phones. We have extremely powerful devices in our pockets and we use them to do astounding things every day.

Took a wrong turn on the freeway? Google Maps will get you back on track. Want to know if that new coffee shop is open yet? Simply open your web browser while you walk down the street. Trying to decide which movie to go to? Go to Rotten Tomatoes while standing in the theatre lobby. These are all things we take for granted now, but 15 years ago, none of this was possible.

We have all become accustomed to getting information when and where we need it and in extremely short bursts, because that's the only way it will be useful in our moment of need.

Micro Idea 10

The second major factor driving microlearning is social media and our social connectedness. Facebook, Twitter, Pinterest... these are all common apps, and even if you don't use all of them, you certainly have an idea of what they do.

We are social animals, and have always learned from each other. My grandmother perfected her cooking every time she visited a neighbor's house and tried a new dish. Now we have Pinterest. What's really going on is no different—we've just widened our circle of friends and found ways to share ideas electronically.

We have always been accustomed to learning from others in short bursts, but now we're becoming accustomed to doing that in electronic environments.

Micro Idea 11

The third major factor driving microlearning is that we are all extremely busy. We're plugged in 24x7 and can access our professional and personal work any time.

When "bag phones" were first coming out 25 years ago my dad famously announced that he would never have a cell phone because his car was his one sanctity where people couldn't reach him on the phone. He cherished his commute time as a time to mentally recharge. How things have changed since then! (My dad now has the latest iPhone.)

With our hyper-connectedness, we feel busier and more pressed for time all day, every day. As a result, we're looking for ways to learn what we need to learn as quickly as possible. We are willing to give up the fullest, richest understanding of a topic to get just the part we need right now.

Micro Idea 12

Because we're learning all the time in our personal lives, we intuitively understand that we can use similar strategies for learning in our professional lives. We have those same mobile devices in our pockets at work, we have the same social structures available at our desks, and there is certainly no place we feel more crunched for time than at work.

This is the flywheel of factors that makes microlearning so hot right now. We saw the power and impact of this learning in our personal lives first, but now it's natural to ask how we can apply it to our work lives. We know we can learn things quickly and in short bursts, and now we want to do that at work too.

Micro Idea 13

If you can address learning needs more quickly and efficiently, employees will be grateful (and so will their managers).

Is microlearning instructionally sound?

Micro Idea 14

In some cases, managers or participants may be demanding that learning be shorter so it can be more effectively layered into the workday. You may be questioning the instructional value of microlearning, but it really can be good for learning.

Micro Idea 15

The forgetting curve tells us that, unless there is an attempt to rehearse or practice, we forget new learning very quickly. Typically people will forget half of what they learned in a class within the first 24 hours and almost everything in a matter of days. (But you probably didn't need research to tell you that—you know it from experience!)

We tell college students that they can't just go to a lecture and expect to ace the final exam months later. But this is pretty much what we expect when we put employees through a training class, or tell them to take an eLearning, and expect that they will work differently as a result.

The forgetting curve is disrupted when we have spaced learning—and nearly obliterated when we have reactivation moments. Microlearning allows us to create both spacing and reactivation (also called repetition), which are critical to effective learning that sticks.

(For more on the forgetting curve as it applies to current learning situations, see Clark Quinn's blog at http://blog.learnlets.com/?p=3321)

Micro Idea 16

Conrad Gottfredson and Bob Mosher found that when you combine learning with performance support, you can cut training in half and reach competency twice as fast. This research supports our use of microlearning.

(For more, see Con and Bob's article at http://www.learningsolutionsmag.com/articles/934/)

Micro Idea 17

The research on spacing, repetition, and performance support clearly support the use of microlearning. This should put your instructional design sensibilities at ease. You can also use this research to justify using microlearning with your team or in your organization.

The Microlearning
Use Case

Micro Idea 18

Now let's look at the use case—that is, when does microlearning fit, and when does it not. We shouldn't use microlearning for *every* learning situation, but there are key times when it will fit very well.

Micro Idea 19

Microlearning is best for material that is already familiar to the learner. Typically these are cases where the learner is reviewing or extending their existing knowledge.

Micro Idea 20

As learning professionals, we often underestimate what our learners already know. People come to us with a lot of existing knowledge and experience already! So microlearning can be used in many cases—for things like annual compliance training, teaching leadership skills, enhancing sales skills, and lots and lots of other things.

Micro Idea 21

Another situation where microlearning is particularly well suited is where there is content that can be isolated into discrete chunks. This is especially relevant to content that aligns with a process or that can otherwise be broken into multiple steps, parts, or concepts.

Micro Idea 22

Microlearning is often not best for material that is new or complicated, especially if it needs to be covered in depth.

Micro Idea 23

There are many ways you can use microlearning:

- Preparation before training
- Follow-up after training
- Standalone training
- Standalone performance support

It is helpful to understand these different areas, but instead of focusing on which one it is, ask "How will I improve performance?" not if it's learning, performance support, mentoring, marketing, or something else.

Micro Idea 24

You can use microlearning **before** training (in any form—instructor-led, eLearning, or virtual instructor-led). Using microlearning prior to training can get people thinking about and used to the new ideas they'll be grappling with in the class. It can also get everyone up to the same level before coming to a live or virtual instructor-led class.

Micro Idea 25

You can use microlearning **after** training (in any form—instructor-led, eLearning, or virtual instructor-led) to create the "pull through" that will make learning more effective and reduce scrap learning.

(Scrap learning is all the things that people *forget* from our training. All that time and effort for us to teach them, and for them to learn it, is essentially scrapped or thrown away.)

Micro Idea 26

Microlearning can stand on its own. It is often used as just-in-time learning or informal learning that follows the learner's needs and interests because the learner is in control of when and what they learn.

We are most familiar with this use of microlearning in our personal lives, where people follow other people or topics and use microlearning content such as blogs and videos to extend their knowledge and thinking. Notice how in this use case the learner is exploring something of interest. They don't have to watch that video or blog, and it's not related to a specific performance goal the learner has at that moment. It's more of an exploratory form of learning.

We can, however, create similar learning in our organizations. Identify a few topics that lots of employees are likely to be interested in—for example, a new selling approach, change management, dealing with difficult customers—and collect a number of resources from which employees can pull.

Micro Idea 27

So far we've talked about stand-alone microlearning being optional, but it can also be required. Imagine your compliance training or other required learning. Cutting it down to a five minute piece or a series of five minute pieces is a great way to show your employees that you care about their time.

Micro Idea 28

Any time someone thinks they know the answer to something, but wants to use a resource to confirm their understanding of it, brush up on the specifics, or practice an example, we are talking about performance support—learning in the moment of need. Microlearning fits very well here because it is bite-sized and directly tied to the thing the person wants to learn.

For example, let's say I'm in the middle of working on a report for my boss using Microsoft Word and I can't get the footers to work the way I want. I can watch a video on YouTube or Lynda.com to find out how to do it, and then go back to my report and apply those new skills right away. Notice how in this use case I wasn't just exploring something of interest. I was specifically learning something that I needed to do my job right now.

How do I go micro?

Micro Idea 29

In going micro, one of the **biggest mistakes** instructional designers make is focusing on the **learning objective** instead of the **performance objective**.

Micro Idea 30

Instructional designers often focus on learning for the sake of learning—but not all learners care about this, and even those who do are time crunched and just need to get their work done.

Micro Idea 31

Adult learners are driven by the performance outcome (the performance improvement they perceive they will get)—and these feelings have become even stronger over the past decade as we've become more plugged in and more time-crunched.

Micro Idea 32

Always ask yourself: **How do I earn every minute of seat time?**

And: **Would I give up my time in a busy day for this learning?**

Micro Idea 33

Use the **Three C's** to help you collect or develop micro resources and the **MILE model** to guide yourself through creating a microlearning program. There are chapters on each of these later in this book.

The Three C's

Micro Idea 34

Use the **Three C's** to help you collect or create your micro content:

- Curate
- Create
- Crowdsource

The order of this list is purposeful. If at all possible, curating your content should be your first choice as it the most efficient. If that isn't possible, then create. And crowdsourcing is a great strategy, but often difficult to achieve in a corporate environment, which is why I've put it last.

Micro Idea 35

When you **curate**, you or your team finds what you think are the "best of the best" resources on the internet—or your intranet if you have a good internal library of content.

Our real goal with a curation strategy is to circumvent people "Googling" the internet or intranet for content. We want to make it more efficient and more reliable!

Micro Idea 36

There's a misconception that curating content is lazy, but it takes careful searching and review to curate quality content. By curating you can create valuable content that helps your employees cut through the clutter on the internet or intranet. This can also focus your employees on resources that align with your corporate philosophies and saves their time.

Micro Idea 37

Instructional designers are always in "create" mode, but I don't recommend creating if content is readily available on the internet. Curating usually finds content that's better than we can produce within our own time and money constraints. It is simply more efficient to curate when possible.

Micro Idea 38

When you **create**, you or your team develop your own nuggets of content from scratch. These generally take the form of blogs, infographics, mini eLearnings, or videos.

Although I recommend curating whenever possible, of course you will need to create materials for internal or proprietary content. You will also need to create if there's something unique about the use of that content in your organization, or if, for any other reason, you need to be able to modify the content or instructional approach.

Micro Idea 39

When you **crowdsource**, people throughout the organization share their favorite resources from the internet or intranet (if you have a good internal library of content).

Micro Idea 40

Crowdsourcing is probably the best use of resources but it is extremely difficult to use in a corporate environment. You need a very large critical mass to make it work. **This is why crowdsourcing works on Facebook and Twitter, but probably doesn't work in your company.**

The one percent rule (also called the 90-9-1 rule) for participation in social media tells us that only one percent of any internet community actively creates new content. An additional nine percent of participants will contribute a little. They may occasionally post new content, but mostly they will like, share, star or favorite other people's content. The remaining 90 percent of the community will only lurk. As a result, you need a very large population for that internet community to be active enough to be valuable for any of the participants. This is why it's so hard to use crowdsourcing within a corporate organization.

(For more on the one percent rule see this article from the Nielsen Norman Group: https://www.nngroup.com/articles/participation-inequality/)

Guidance for Creating or Curating Micro Resources

Micro Idea 41

What makes a good micro resource? Consider this overall guidance for curating or creating your micro resources:

- Single topic focus
- Single audience focus (if possible)
- Brief and to the point
- Strong WIIFM* up-front and throughout
- Eye-catching title—that's your first impression!
- Informal but succinct
- Graphics instead of text
- Must be engaging!

*The WIIFM, or "What's In It For Me" is the motivational element behind the learning. Why should learners care about this content, and why should they take their valuable time to go through it.

Micro Idea 42

Blogs should be easily skim-able. Nothing is more intimidating to learners than a page full of text. Headers, numbered lists, short paragraphs, and bullets will make it easy for the learner to find just what they need. It will also enable them to come back to your blog as a reference resource at any time.

Micro Idea 43

Blogs should use images where possible. A picture really is worth a thousand words, and can be especially helpful when illustrating a point or creating an analogy.

Micro Idea 44

Overall, a blog should be clear and easy to understand. Avoid jargon and make sure you are not unnecessarily complex. Short sentences and paragraphs are also very helpful.

In addition, make sure that every paragraph is relevant. Keep focused and don't go off on tangents, even if you think they are interesting.

Micro Idea 45

Infographics should have a laser focus on a single topic.

Micro Idea 46

A successful infographic keeps the copy brief. If you find yourself writing paragraphs rather than phrases, a blog might be better.

Micro Idea 47

Infographics are meant to take complex concepts and make them simple, so keep the design simple by using lots of white space. Also, use strong images, symbols, and visual metaphors. An infographic is about presenting information through images rather than text.

Micro Idea 48

Infographics should use headers to create visual hierarchy and should have a good flow. Like a good blog, the infographic should guide the reader through a story.

Micro Idea 49

Use video where it adds the most value. Video destroys the learner's ability to self-pace*, so it's important that you're using video in ways that add value to the learner.

*Self-pacing is the idea that the learner is in control of the pace and amount of time they spend with the content. For example, a learner could skim a blog or could read it in more depth to get what they need, based on their own background knowledge and experience, and their time constraints right now.

Micro Idea 50

Video is great for explaining a process or procedure because there are multiple steps that happen over time. If that process is highly physical, video is sure to have a significant advantage. For example, using text to explain how to use a hula hoop would be confusing, but using video could be very clear.

Micro Idea 51

Another time when video makes a lot of sense is situations where audio and visual are important together, such as how to find a stud on the wall.

Micro Idea 52

Video is ideal for showing relationships or dialog between people. It's also your go-to medium for showing emotion. Video really should be your first choice if the content has an emotional element. For example, you can make a very strong case for the need to follow safety guidelines using video—interview a person who was hurt at work because they did not follow the safety guidelines. Hearing another person's heartfelt words and seeing their expressions will have a significant impact that you just can't get in a blog or infographic.

(An outstanding example of this is this PSA for how to put out a kitchen grease fire: https://www.youtube.com/watch?v=Bh5WnbBx7XI)

Micro Idea 53

If you decide to use video, remember that a story will always be more memorable than bullets of text onscreen. It's not just that the story is engaging—it's that our brain remembers stories more easily than discrete facts.

And even if your content seems very text-heavy, you can add pictures and scenarios to make it more story-like.

Micro Idea 54

Remember that the power of your message is always more important than the medium you choose—blog, infographic, or video.

The MILE Model:
A Model for Microlearning

Micro Idea 55

What if you want...

- More than just a single micro resource?
- A stream of micro pieces that work together?
- To address one or more performance objectives?

How do you develop a microlearning program?

Micro Idea 56

We need a roadmap for taking a course and making it micro.

Micro Idea 57

ADDIE is a solid instructional design model, but there are issues because it's linear, and because it focusses us on the learning objectives but not necessarily performance.

Micro Idea 58

To create a microlearning program you need a laser focus on your performance objectives and how you can address them in bite-sized pieces.

Micro Idea 59

To create a good microlearning program we need an iterative model that is focused on performance. We need a different model to support different thinking—we need to use the MILE model instead of ADDIE.

Micro Idea 60

Create or Select Resources

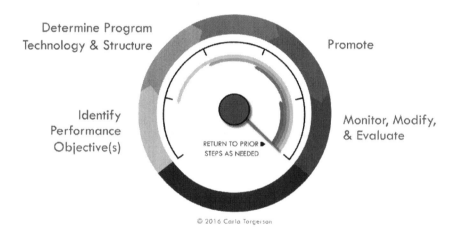

Determine Program
Technology & Structure

Promote

Identify
Performance
Objective(s)

Monitor, Modify,
& Evaluate

RETURN TO PRIOR ▶
STEPS AS NEEDED

© 2016 Carla Torgerson

Micro Idea 61

The MILE model is designed to look like speedometer and a car travelling a mile.

How long does it take to drive a mile?

Of course it depends on the speed you travel, which is dependent on the road conditions, the driver, the car, the weather, and a host of other factors. But overall, it takes about one to five minutes to drive a mile.

Similarly, the length for any microlearning resource will depend on a number of factors—the audience, the content, the technology, and a host of other factors. But overall, the optimal length of a microlearning resource is about one to five minutes.

Micro Idea 62

When we use the MILE model we have a number of steps that we go through. The steps of the MILE model are:

- Step 1: Identify Performance Objective(s)
- Step 2: Determine Program Technology and Structure
- Step 3: Create or Select Resources
- Step 4: Promote
- Step 5: Monitor, Modify, and Evaluate

Micro Idea 63

The MILE model is an iterative model, not a linear one, so you can quickly jump back and forth to any step at any time. Like a speedometer, you can quickly move the needle anywhere you want. This enables you to continually improve the program to ensure outstanding results.

Just like a speedometer, if you revisit an earlier step you are not moving backward—you may feel like you're slowing down, but you're always moving forward.

Micro Idea 64

Current trends are to use iterative instructional design models. The most prevalent ones are Michael Allen's SAM model and Megan Torrance's LLAMA model.

We want to be iterative with instructional design for live and eLearning delivery, but with microlearning it's even more feasible because each piece of instruction is so small that we can revise it very quickly and easily. This may be our opportunity to finally be as agile as possible!

MILE Step 1: Identify Performance Objective(s)

Micro Idea 65

The first step of the MILE model is to identify the performance objective(s).

Micro Idea 66

The first question you should ask yourself as you create your microlearning program is: **What will they come away with?**

This could be a knowledge objective but generally we want a performance objective—that is, something the learner will be able to do differently as a result of using this microlearning program.

Micro Idea 67

To be able to properly do this step you also need to know the audience—
who will use this program and see this change in performance. You want
a good sense of this, but don't spend a lot of time on the audience
analysis. Focus on the performance objective and your understanding of
the audience should become apparent.

Micro Idea 68

If your performance objective is small, then you are finished with this step of the MILE model.

But if the objective is bigger (which most are), you'll need to break that objective down into the terminal and enabling learning objectives, just like you would for a four hour in-person class or a 30 minute piece of eLearning.

Micro Idea 69

The terminal objective is your performance objective—it's what learners will be able to do differently as a result of the program.

The enabling objectives are what learners need to know or be able to do to get there. These are really the "building blocks" of the learning.

Micro Idea 70

Enabling objectives are critical. They help us to make learning bite-sized.

Micro Idea 71

Converting a class into microlearning can be difficult because, when we think of classes, we usually focus on learning objectives and how all the pieces flow together.

We don't usually have a performance objective for every section of the class, and maybe not even for the entire program.

Micro Idea 72

When we go micro, our focus shifts from having a good flow to having a series of performance-focused objectives.

Even with good enabling objectives for your microlearning program, it's easy to lose sight of performance. Remember that the enabling objectives need to be performance-focused if at all possible!

Micro Idea 73

You shouldn't take a one hour course and divide it into 12 five minute chunks that need to be consumed in sequence. Instead, identify the enabling objectives and create one micro module for each one. This will make the learning more actionable for the learner.

Micro Idea 74

The more specific the enabling objectives, the easier it will be to think about that content in a bite-sized way.

Micro Idea 75

For example, let's say I wanted to teach consultative selling skills to sales reps.

Terminal Objective:

Employees will be able to use consultative selling skills with potential customers.

Enabling Objectives:

Employees will be able to[*]:

- Research the client
- Ask good questions
- Listen effectively
- Teach about our product
- Qualify the opportunity
- Close the sale

[*]The enabling objectives in this example are pretty broad. It may help you to think even more granularly and create even more specific enabling objectives.

(These enabling objectives come from "The Consultative Sales Process" at http://blog.hubspot.com/customers/bid/172099/the-consultative-sales-process-6-principles)

Micro Idea 76

To continue our example, here's what a microlearning program on consultative selling could look like. It could be posted on your intranet or social collaborative platform (such as Yammer or Jive), or even on your LMS.

Consultative Selling

① Research the client.	② Ask good questions.	③ Listen effectively.
• Blog (2 pages): 5 Ways to Research Your Potential Customers • Video (3:12): Research Your Client's Market & Product Strategy **Application**: Pick two techniques from the above resources that you think will really work for you. Use them as consistently as possible for the next two weeks.	• Infographic (2 pages): 10 Tips For Asking More Effective Sales Questions • Blog (1 page): 23 Sales Questions To Quickly Identify Your Customer's Core Needs **Application**: Write down three questions that apply to most of your prospects. Use them as often as possible and hone them over the next three weeks.	• Blog: (2 pages): 6 Important Tips for Becoming a Better Listener in Sales • Video (4:03) Effective Listening Skills **Application**: Pick just one listening technique and use it as consistently as possible for just one week. Then the next week add one more technique. Add a new technique every week for a month.

MILE Step 2: Determine Program Technology and Structure

Micro Idea 77

The second step of the MILE model is to determine the program technology and structure.

Micro Idea 78

Now that you know the performance goal (and audience), you need to figure out the best way to target that group's needs. Ask questions like these:

Technology:

- Will it be video- or text/image-based?
- Will it be on an LMS or somewhere else?
- Will it be tracked?
- Will it be required?

Structure:

- Is this preparation, follow-up, stand-alone training, or performance support? (see "The Microlearning Use Case" chapter earlier in this book)
- Is this formal or informal learning?
- How expert are the learners?
- What types of resources will you use (video, text, image)?
- Will resources be released all at once or in a continuous stream?
- How long will the resources be?

In some ways, technology and structure are very different, but they are so interrelated that they need to be determined together.

Micro Idea 79

Videos and animations destroy the learner's ability to self-pace*. As a result, even with microlearning, the more expert the learners are, the more they will prefer text with graphics to video or animation. Micro resources that are text- or image-based allow them to get just what they need and skip over what they already know.

*As discussed earlier, self-pacing is the idea that the learner is in control of their pace and the amount of time that they spend with the content.

Micro Idea 80

Use more text-based resources for audiences that are more time crunched or whose time is most important to the organization (for example, higher level leaders, commission-based employees, very specialized or highly paid employees). These are people for whom self-pacing is very important.

Micro Idea 81

So, in our consultative selling example, we could make these decisions:

Technology:

- Content housed on a Yammer page (social collaborative system)
- Always have two resource formats (text, infographic, video), and never more than six resources total
- Learning is not required
- Usage is not tracked
- You can earn completion credit on the LMS

Structure:

- Standalone training
- Completely informal and optional
- Learners have a mixed amount of expertise
- Mix of text, infographic, and video resources
- Release the entire program at one time
- No resources longer than five minutes (sales reps will prefer them to be as short as possible!)

MILE Step 3: Create or Select Resources

Micro Idea 82

The third step of the MILE model is to create or select resources.

Micro Idea 83

Remember from the first step of the MILE model that if you have multiple enabling objectives, they will be the "sections" of the program. If you have only one enabling objective, it will be the program. But don't lose sight of performance.

Micro Idea 84

Recall our earlier example of teaching consultative selling skills to sales reps. Here are our objectives:

Terminal Objective:

Employees will be able to use consultative selling skills with potential customers.

Enabling Objectives:

Employees will be able to:

- Research the client.
- Ask good questions.
- Listen effectively.
- Teach about our product.
- Qualify the opportunity.
- Close the sale.

(These enabling objectives come from "The Consultative Sales Process" at http://blog.hubspot.com/customers/bid/172099/the-consultative-sales-process-6-principles)

Micro Idea 85

Take a look at the example on the previous page. Can we teach everything about "researching the client" in five minutes? No way. Could we teach something important about "researching the client" in five minutes? Of course. And that's the point here—you don't have to teach everything about a concept. But what is something that the learner would find valuable?

Micro Idea 86

In a microlearning program the enabling objectives will become the sections of the program. In each section you will provide a few microlearning resources that address the enabling objective.

Micro Idea 87

Next you need to curate, create, or crowdsource the content. For each enabling objective, identify one or more resources that will each take no more than five minutes to address that enabling objective.

Micro Idea 88

If you curate or crowdsource your content it will be fairly easy to identify the "good" resources.

If you create your content, refer to the "Guidance for Creating or Curating Micro Resources" chapter earlier in this book for recommendations.

Micro Idea 89

If you are creating a micro resource, have just one enabling objective and address it as concisely as possible.

Micro Idea 90

If you are creating a micro resource, always ask yourself:

- What are the **most critical** thing(s) to being able to **do** this behavior?
- How do I **earn every minute** of seat time?
- Would I give up **my time** in a busy day for this learning?

Micro Idea 91

As you are creating or collecting your microlearning resources, make sure that every resource has a direct link to performance. If you don't have a clear and direct WIIFM* in each resource, the learner will consider the resource a waste of time—even if it is only five minutes long.

*As discussed earlier, the WIIFM, or "What's In It For Me" is the motivational element behind the learning.

MILE Step 4: Promote

Micro Idea 92

The fourth step of the MILE model is to promote your program.

Micro Idea 93

After you have the resources created or selected, it's easy! Well, sort of.

Post the resources on your social platform or LMS (as you had decided in Step 2: Determine Program Technology and Structure). That's the easy part—but then you also have to promote the content.

Micro Idea 94

Remember that with a lot of microlearning programs, the learning is not required, so it's critical to keep that content top of mind with your learners.

If learning is required, we can force learners to go to the LMS and take a class. And if they don't complete it we can pepper them (and their managers) with reminders or threats until they do.

But with learning that is not required, it's much harder to get people to consume the materials—the learners are in control, so they choose what they want to learn and when. This is where learning professionals have to start thinking like marketers to get people to consume their content.

Micro Idea 95

Promoting the program (marketing) is the step that most instructional designers are weakest at! As a result, I have a number of tips and ideas in this chapter to help you promote your content.

Micro Idea 96

If they don't **know** it exists, they **can't** use it.

If they don't **remember** it exists, they **won't** use it.

Micro Idea 97

You could have the **best** microlearning program in the world, but if people **don't know** it exists, or if they **can't find** what they need when they need it, **they won't use it**.

Micro Idea 98

Keeping your content top of mind is critical. Find ways to continually alert your audience that the resources are available—and use as many communication channels as possible.

Micro Idea 99

Here are just a few ways that you can let people know your materials exist:

- Post banner ads on your LMS or social collaborative system
- Send emails to potential participants
- Link from your department website or intranet page
- List the program in your course catalog or LMS
- Share a QR code leading to your learning portal or microlearning program
- Post a blog about it on your social collaborative system
- Tell people about it in classes (live and eLearning)
- Better yet, use it in the classes
- Send flyers
- Put up posters
- Put table tents in common areas
- Give away marketing "swag" such as pens, post-it notes, mouse pads, etc. that people will use at their desks every day

Micro Idea 100

I believe there is a strong correlation between promoting microlearning content and marketing strategies, especially if the microlearning program is not required.

Micro Idea 101

What can we learn from how marketers promote a website? Foremost is that search engine optimization is critical. This is the use of keywords, headers, and meta tags. Make sure you know how the system that will house your microlearning program indexes pages!

Sources (for the ideas here and on the next few pages):

Wilson, The Web Marketing Checklist: 37 Ways to Promote Your Website, http://www.practicalecommerce.com/articles/99540-checklist

Pozin, 10 Proven Ways to Market Your Website, http://www.forbes.com/sites/ilyapozin/2012/04/11/10-proven-ways-to-market-your-website

Micro Idea 102

Linking from other pages is also very important. Think of all the other pages you own that your learners might visit. And can you get other people to link to your site? Those links from outside become endorsements for your content!

Micro Idea 103

What are some of the social media tactics marketers use to get you to engage with their content? Here are just a few:

- Blog about the topic or your specific content
- Participate in online social communities so you become a trusted source of content
- Create ways for other people to talk about your materials in social channels—people look to friends and colleagues for recommended content
- Provide new content that gets people interacting with your content on a regular basis. This is often done using blogs, tweets, and emails

Micro Idea 104

Here are some other suggestions for marketing techniques you can use to promote your microlearning program:

- Include your URL in any print materials
- Mention your microlearning program in classes
- Add the URL to your email signature
- Give away free stuff—for example, give something to the first ten people to complete the program, or have a random drawing from all the people who complete the program within a certain time period
- Do something to create buzz—here's where marketers try to create something that goes viral. Can you create a blog or tweet about your program that is so catchy that people forward it because it's just so cool or interesting?
- Send direct emails to potential learners

Micro Idea 105

Being able to easily search for your content is critical. This is especially true for content that is easy to Google or not required for learners to complete. In those cases, if learners can't easily find your microlearning content, they will go to Google or just skip it.

Micro Idea 106

Where you host the materials must have excellent search, and make sure you tag your content so your tool will index the pages well.

Micro Idea 107

A lot of our tools don't have search that is even close to as good as Google—and that puts us at a disadvantage. Find out how your tool indexes pages so you can improve searchability.

Micro Idea 108

Find ways to organize your content so that people don't have to hunt for it. For example, creating a microlearning library or portal can be a great way to get people to your content quickly.

Usability and Stickiness: Getting People to Keep Coming Back

Micro Idea 109

If you create a portal, make sure you organize the content in a way that matches how the audience would use that content in their work. Often, instructional designers will organize content differently than the actual user. Make sure you follow what the user would instinctively want. A portal is intended to make it easier for the user to find content, not harder.

Micro Idea 110

For learning that is not required, you should create a program where people want to stay for a while and keep coming back. Marketers call this creating "sticky" content.

Micro Idea 111

There is lots of great guidance from the marketing field about how to make a site "sticky":

- Make sure the page or site navigation is intuitive
- Make sure the text is readable on any browser and device the employee may use
- Continually add fresh content
- Let people subscribe to your content
- Include your personality in your content—make it fun and inviting

Source (for the ideas here and on the next page):

DeMers, 20 Sticky Features Your Website Needs to Convert Visitors, http://www.forbes.com/sites/jaysondemers/2014/07/29/20-sticky-features-your-website-needs-to-convert-visitors

Micro Idea 112

Here is additional guidance from the marketing field about how to make a site "sticky":

- Allow the reader to engage with your content by posting and responding to comments
- Create a highlight reel of your most popular micro-programs
- Have a competition or free offer
- Include user testimonials and reviews (it establishes credibility, especially for new users)
- List your awards and accomplishments
- Provide a tease into similar content (for example, have links to other related content at the end of a blog or microlearning program)

Micro Idea 113

As you read the guidance for making a site "sticky" on the last two pages, think about your experiences on Amazon.com. Amazon's marketers are masters at almost all of these techniques—and it absolutely gets you to stay longer and consume more content.

Think about how you can use strategies similar to Amazon's to get learners to keep coming back to your microlearning content.

Micro Idea 114

Make your site so usable that people keep coming back:

- Content is quick and easy to consume
- Employees find answers to their specific questions/needs quickly
- It is easy to "re-find" a resource in the moment of need
- Content is available on their primary device when they have a spare moment at work
- Content is integrated with the flow of work, if possible

Micro Idea 115

The more that learners can get what they need when they need it, the more they'll use it. Searchability and usability are paramount.

MILE Step 5: Monitor, Modify, and Evaluate

Micro Idea 116

The fifth, and final, step of the MILE model is to monitor, modify, and evaluate the program. However, remember that MILE is an iterative model, so any time you see something that's not working well, you should quickly revisit a previous step of the model.

Micro Idea 117

Ideally, your program should be posted in a place that allows the user to add comments, likes, and shares. Monitor that user data and use it to evaluate and modify the program.

Micro Idea 118

Often, we think about posting our content in an LMS. However, consider posting your content on a social collaborative system if you have one. All social systems allow people to comment, like, and share content, while few LMSs do. Consider carefully if the social system might be a better fit for your microlearning program.

Micro Idea 119

If the completion of the microlearning program needs to be tracked, an LMS will be the best place for your content.

But if the learning is informal (that is, it's optional and can be completed at any time), a social collaborative system will often be the best place for your content because it allows people to add comments, likes, and shares.

Make sure you post your content in the place that enables you to get the data you need most.

Micro Idea 120

Whatever tool you use, watch your metrics data. For example, usage numbers can tell you if people find your program, or any given resource, helpful.

Micro Idea 121

When you look at your evaluation data (metrics data or social comments) ask yourself:

What things are working that you can **repeat**?

What things are not working that you need to **change**?

Micro Idea 122

If you have curated your content from the external web, validate your links often. Broken links are one of the fastest ways to drive users away from your program.

The good news, though, is that it's easy to quickly click the links on a page and ensure they all work. And if there are any broken links, you can quickly replace them with new curated resources.

Micro Idea 123

With microlearning, formal evaluation like quizzes should generally be avoided. Imagine consuming two or three minutes of content and then having to take a quiz! It's clunky, and unless learners see a business purpose (such as a compliance requirement) it may cause them to avoid your content in the future.

Micro Idea 124

A lot of microlearning is informal learning, so we generally focus more on usage metrics than test scores. So we need to start thinking of the metrics used by marketers rather than those used by learning professionals.

Micro Idea 125

Looking at the metrics that marketers commonly track to measure the effectiveness of a website, these are the ones that apply well to measuring microlearning programs:

- Unique visitors (the number of people who visit your site)
- Page views (the number of hits to any of your pages)
- Bounce rate (the percentage of visitors who come to your page and immediately "bounce" or leave)
- Time spent (the amount of time a person spends on a page or the entire site)
- Number of comments
- Number of likes or shares

Source:

Cain, Measuring Marketing Effectiveness, http://contentmarketinginstitute.com/2012/10/measuring-marketing-effectiveness-metrics/

Micro Idea 126

If a microlearning program is not required, it's critical to track the number of unique visitors and the number of page views.

The number of unique visitors is your best indication of overall usage— how well is the promotion of the microlearning program working?

The bounce rate (percentage of people who come to your page and leave immediately) is also an indicator of how well your marketing is representing your page. This is excellent data, but can be hard to get from typical tools used by learning professionals (like an LMS or social system).

Micro Idea 127

The number of page views tells you the number of pages within your site that people go to. If the number of page views is higher than the number of unique visitors, it tells you that a single person is accessing more than one page and/or the person is coming back to the same page multiple times.

Either situation is a positive sign, and you can do further analysis to determine which case is happening. It can be helpful to know if someone found a single page or resource so helpful that they kept going back to it.

Micro Idea 128

Deeper analytics are possible if you use xAPI to track your data. Then you can also consider things like the number of links on your page that are clicked on, in what order, and even if a person clicks on the same link multiple times.

Micro Idea 129

Although I see it as secondary, I'd be remiss if I didn't talk about assessing learning for a moment. While most microlearning is informal learning, there are many situations where it is important to track completion or a score on the training. A prime example of this is compliance training.

Here are a few approaches, many of which you're probably using already:

- LMS completion credit
- Badging based on completion
- Post-test (immediately or 30-days post)
- Pre-test / post-test combination
- Gamification—have learners "play a game" at the end of the microlearning, and track their score on the game
- When you gamify, you can even have leaderboards so people can compare themselves to each other

Of course, the best option here would be to look at performance on the job. Did the learner's behavior change in the ways you wanted?

Lessons Learned

Micro Idea 130

My biggest lessons learned from creating microlearning programs are on the following pages. I'm sure you'll have your own. Scribble them in this section so you don't forget them!

Micro Idea 131

The shorter the resource, the better.

Micro Idea 132

Even a short piece of content will feel long if it's not designed well or if it doesn't meet the learner's specific need.

Micro Idea 133

Video destroys the learner's ability to self-pace. Unless there's a compelling reason to use video, use text and/or images instead.

Micro Idea 134

Interest in your microlearning program may be very strong initially, but it will wane quickly if you don't continue to market it.

Micro Idea 135

You should promote your programs regularly while you build a library of microlearning programs.

Micro Idea 136

If the learning is not required, offer "course credit" for those who want it. Provide an optional completion form where people can answer questions about how they applied the content to their work. When they submit it, mark them complete on the LMS.

Micro Idea 137

Searchability is critical. If people can't find your content, they won't use it.

Micro Idea 138

Engaging leaders or teams to work through a program together is powerful in creating accountability!

Conclusion

Micro Idea 139

Microlearning can be good for learning. We can meet learners' needs quickly and focus on performance—which is what they really care about.

Micro Idea 140

Microlearning should empower anyone who designs instruction and make our jobs fun! It shouldn't feel like we're churning out garbage, but rather like we're making a difference.

Micro Idea 141

Ask yourself this: What's just one thing you read in this book that you will commit to trying in your next project? Actually find one thing, and write it here. If you write it down, you're more likely to do it.

And please send me your comments, feedback, and suggestions. **You can reach me at carla@torgersonconsulting.com.**

Made in the USA
Middletown, DE
01 September 2018